www.FlowerpotPress.com
PAB-0808-0288
ISBN: 978-1-4867-1793-4
Made in China/Fabriqué en Chine

HORNS

Katrine Crow

Who has
CURVED HORNS
like these?

An alpine ibex!

Who has
POINTY HORNS
like these?

A banteng!

Who has RIDGED HORNS like these?

A gazelle!

Who has
SPIRAL HORNS
like these?

A markhor!

Who has STRONG HORNS like these?

A rhino!

Who has
THREE HORNS
like these?

A jackson's chameleon!

Who has
LONG HORNS
like these?

A highland cow!